from SEA TO SHINING SEA
MICHIGAN

By Dennis Brindell Fradin

CONSULTANT

Robert L. Hillerich, Ph.D., Consultant, Pinellas County Schools, Florida;
Visiting Professor, University of South Florida

CHILDRENS PRESS®
CHICAGO

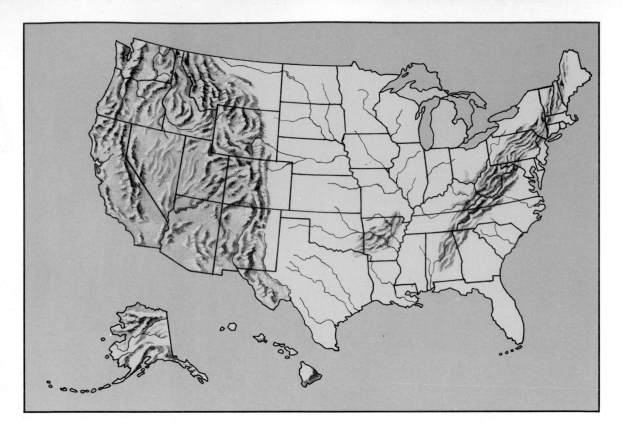

Michigan is one of the twelve states in the region called the Midwest. The other Midwest states are Illinois, Indiana, Iowa, Kansas, Minnesota, Missouri, Nebraska, North Dakota, Ohio, South Dakota, and Wisconsin.

For my aunt, Frances Fradin Oscodar

For her help, the author thanks Elizabeth Giese, Education Director, Michigan Women's Historical Center and Hall of Fame, Lansing.

Front cover picture, Renaissance Center, Detroit; page 1, Point Betsie Lighthouse; back cover, Pictured Rocks National Lakeshore, Upper Peninsula

Project Editor: Joan Downing
Design Director: Karen Kohn
Research Assistant: Judith Bloom Fradin
Typesetting: Graphic Connections, Inc.
Engraving: Liberty Photoengraving

THIRD PRINTING, 1994.

Library of Congress Cataloging-in-Publication Data

Fradin, Dennis B.
  Michigan / by Dennis Brindell Fradin.
    p. cm. — (From sea to shining sea)
  Includes index.
  Summary: An introduction to the Wolverine State, its history, economy, cities, and people.
  ISBN 0-516-03822-2
  1. Michigan—Juvenile literature. [1. Michigan.] I. Title II. Series: Fradin, Dennis B. From sea to shining sea.
  F566.3.F68 1992   91-32920
  977.4—dc20   CIP
                                                    AC

Table of Contents

Costumed children enjoying the Holland Tulip Festival parade

INTRODUCING THE WOLVERINE STATE

Michigan is a beautiful state in the region called the Midwest. It is a leader in both manufacturing and farming. Michigan's beaches and ski trails make the state a popular vacationland.

A peninsula is a piece of land that is almost surrounded by water.

Michigan has two separate parts. The Lower Peninsula is to the south. The Upper Peninsula is to the north. It is called the U. P., for short.

The state's name comes from *Michigama*, a Chippewa Indian word meaning "great lake." That was the Chippewa name for Lake Michigan.

Fur traders were among Michigan's first non-Indians. Some of them traded wolverine furs. Because of this, Michigan is called the "Wolverine State."

Today, millions of Americans drive cars made in Michigan. They also eat fruit grown in Michigan.

The Wolverine State is special in many other ways. Where is the world's number-one city for making breakfast cereals? Where was famous singer Diana Ross born? Where did President Gerald Ford grow up? The answer to all these questions is: Michigan!

*Overleaf: Carp River,
Porcupine Mountain
Wilderness State Park*

*A picture map
of Michigan*

DUNNINGTON

A Varied Geography

A Varied Geography

The country of Canada is north of the United States—in most places. Much of Michigan, however, is north of the Canada-U.S. border. Besides Canada and four of the Great Lakes, Michigan is bordered by the states of Ohio, Indiana, and Wisconsin.

Michigan has flatlands, hills, and mountains. It has beaches, islands, forests, and even swamps.

Geographers divide the state into two regions. The western half of the Upper Peninsula is part of

Four of the five Great Lakes touch Michigan. They are Lakes Erie, Huron, Superior (below), and Michigan.

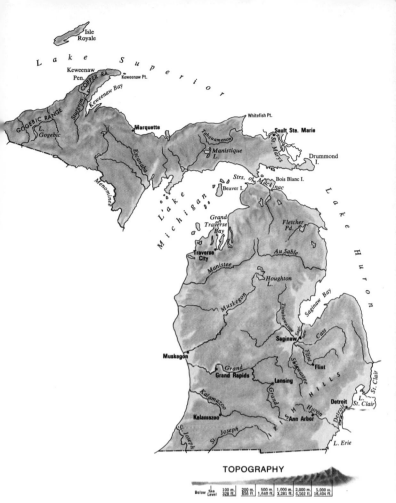

the Superior Upland. This is the state's mountainous area. Michigan's highest point is in this region. It is 1,979-foot tall Mount Arvon.

The Lower Peninsula and the eastern half of the Upper Peninsula are part of the Great Lakes Plains. The plains are lowlands that are hilly in places.

Many islands in the Great Lakes are part of Michigan. The largest is Isle Royale, in Lake Superior. Other islands include Mackinac, in Lake Huron, and Beaver, in Lake Michigan.

Isle Royale (above) is closer to Canada than it is to the mainland of Michigan.

9

Left: Fall color on a wooded road in the Upper Peninsula Right: Virgin white pines in Hartwick Pines State Park

About half of Michigan is forest. Birches, maples, oaks, pines, and spruces grow in Michigan's woodlands. Much of the Upper Peninsula is forested. In some places, hikers can see nothing but forest for days.

Michigan's climate is rather cool, especially in the Upper Peninsula. The two peninsulas can have very different weather on the same day. For example,

it may be 85 degrees Fahrenheit in Detroit on a June day while the Upper Peninsula is only 55 degrees Fahrenheit. Winter temperatures sometimes dip below minus 20 degrees Fahrenheit in the Upper Peninsula. The Upper Peninsula is also famous for its huge snowfalls. People in the Upper Peninsula have been known to tunnel through the snow to get out of their homes.

Summer at Au Train Bay, Lake Superior

From Ancient Times
Until Today

FROM ANCIENT TIMES UNTIL TODAY

Many millions of years ago, Michigan was much different than it is today. At times, volcanoes erupted in the area. Now and then, shallow seas covered Michigan. When the seas dried, they left two gifts for Michigan: salt and oil.

About two million years ago, the Ice Age began. Huge sheets of ice called glaciers moved down from the north. They covered all of Michigan. The glaciers dug holes in the ground. The holes later filled with water. The largest holes became the Great Lakes. The smaller holes became the thousands of smaller lakes that dot Michigan.

During the Ice Age, woolly mammoths and mastodons lived in Michigan. They were related to our modern elephants. Beavers that were as big as an adult person also lived in Michigan.

If all the salt in Michigan were mined, it would supply the earth for thousands of years.

AMERICAN INDIANS

Prehistoric Indians reached Michigan at least twelve thousand years ago. The early Indians hunted deer and moose. About four thousand years ago, the

Opposite: Workers on a Ford assembly line putting together Model T automobiles

13

American Indians in northern regions invented snowshoes for winter travel. This Chippewa is wearing snowshoes while he hunts for deer.

Furs obtained from the Indians were made into fancy clothes in Europe.

Indians began mining copper in the Upper Peninsula. Isle Royale has ruins of an ancient copper mine. The Indians used the copper to make knives and spear tips.

Many American Indians, or Native Americans, lived in Michigan in more-recent times. The Chippewas and Menominees were tribes of the Upper Peninsula. The Ottawas, Miamis, and Potawatomis were tribes of the Lower Peninsula. The Wyandot Indians lived on both peninsulas at different times.

Most of these American Indians lived in dome-shaped huts called wigwams. Everyone in the family helped provide food. Women grew corn, beans, and squash. Children gathered berries and wild rice. Men hunted deer and bears with bows and arrows. The Indians used animal skins to make their clothing and blankets.

FRENCH RULE

The French were the first non-Indians in Michigan. France began settling Canada in 1604. They called it New France. Frenchmen came to New France to trade for furs with the Indians. French priests came to teach the Indians about Christianity.

People in New France grew curious about lands to the south. Around 1618, Frenchman Étienne Brulé went out exploring from New France. Brulé reached the Upper Peninsula. He became the first known European in Michigan. In 1634, French explorer Jean Nicolet also reached the Upper Peninsula. Brulé and Nicolet saw that Michigan was rich in furs. France claimed Michigan.

French priests came to Michigan from Canada. In 1660, Father René Ménard built a mission at Keweenaw Bay. Father Jacques Marquette founded a mission at Sault Sainte Marie in 1668. (The name is pronounced SOO SAINT MUH-REE.) This mission was Michigan's first permanent non-Indian settlement. French fur traders also came to Michigan. They traded with the Indians. The French gave the Indians tools in exchange for valuable furs.

The French built a fort at St. Ignace during the 1680s. It became a great fur-trading center known

This statue of Father Jacques Marquette is on Mackinac Island.

The French built Fort Michilimackinac at Mackinaw City in 1715. Like Fort De Buade, it became a fur-trading center. The fort has been reconstructed, and costumed guides such as these show visitors what life was like in the fur-trading days.

as Fort De Buade. In 1694, the governor of New France assigned Antoine de la Mothe Cadillac to command Fort De Buade.

Cadillac earned a fortune in the fur trade at Fort De Buade. He also had an idea. He decided that a place the French called Detroit would be a good spot for a settlement. In 1699, Cadillac went to France. There, King Louis XIV approved his plan.

In mid-1701, Cadillac led about two hundred men and a boy out of Montreal, Canada. The boy was Antoine Cadillac, the commander's nine-year-old son. The group traveled by canoe. It took a few weeks for them to reach the Detroit River. In late July, Cadillac chose a spot on the river to build Detroit. It became a big fur-trading center.

Cadillac hoped that many French people would come to Michigan. Few French people moved to Michigan, though. By 1750, only about a thousand French settlers and soldiers were in Michigan. Nearly all of them were in the Detroit area.

ENGLISH RULE

England was the main country to settle what is now the United States. By the mid-1700s, England ruled thirteen colonies. England and France wanted each

Detroit is a French word meaning "strait." A strait is a narrow body of water that connects two larger bodies of water. Two hundred years after Antoine de la Mothe Cadillac founded Detroit, an automobile was named for him.

other's North American lands. From 1754 to 1763, the two countries fought over control of North America. Because many Indians helped France, the war is called the French and Indian War. Thousands of American colonists helped England.

By late 1760, the English had beaten the French in Canada. It was clear that England would win the war. The English sent some fighting men called Rogers' Rangers to take Michigan. The French gave up Detroit to the Rangers without a fight on November 29, 1760. The French flag over Detroit came down. England's flag was raised in its place. This ended a century of weak French rule in Michigan.

Michigan's few settlers didn't much care who ruled the region. But the change upset the Indians. The French had been more interested in furs than in land. The English took the Indians' land wherever they went in America. Indians in a large area including Michigan fought the English in 1763. An Ottawa chief named Pontiac was one of the Indian leaders. This clash is called Pontiac's War.

The Indians seized fort after fort in Michigan. They soon held every Michigan fort except the one at Detroit. Pontiac hoped for help from the French. But the French did not arrive. The Indians had to

The Rangers (above) were led by Major Robert Rogers of New Hampshire.

17

give up the fight in late 1763. The English reclaimed Michigan.

The English in Michigan were like the French in one way. They were more interested in fur trading than in building towns and farms. As of 1770, there were only about two thousand settlers in Michigan. By then, England was about to lose its American territories.

THE ROAD TO STATEHOOD

England needed money to pay for the French and Indian War. In 1764, England began taxing the Americans to raise money. The Americans were very angry. In 1775, they began fighting the Revolutionary War. They fought the war to break free of England.

Some Michigan Indians fought on the English side. They raided American settlements in Ohio and Pennsylvania. But Michigan's role in the war was small. Most of the fighting took place in the thirteen colonies in the East.

The Americans won the Revolutionary War in 1783. All of Michigan was supposed to come under American rule. But the English didn't give up all their Michigan forts to the Americans until 1796.

Michigan did not become a state for many more years. It was a territory—land owned by the United States. Very few people went to live in Michigan at first. By 1820, its population was just 9,000. Then, over the next several years, huge numbers of people came to Michigan. By 1840, its population was 212,000. That was more than twenty-three times what it had been in 1820!

Better travel routes led to the population boom. In 1825, the Erie Canal opened. The canal cut across New York State. East Coast people could then reach Michigan by boat. Pioneer families traveled along the canal to Buffalo. From there, they traveled on Lake Erie to Detroit. Thousands of easterners came by boat to Michigan. Thousands more came by wagon over dirt roads. Michigan's first railroad was built in the 1830s.

As people moved to Michigan, they built new towns. Ann Arbor, Kalamazoo, Saginaw, and Grand Rapids were begun in the 1820s.

By 1835, Michigan had enough people to become a state. But first, the United States government wanted to end an argument between Michigan and Ohio. The two neighbors were fighting over a piece of land called the Toledo Strip. The dispute was solved in 1836. The Toledo Strip went

A boat being towed on the Erie Canal

19

to Ohio. The Upper Peninsula became part of Michigan. Michigan became the twenty-sixth state on January 26, 1837. Stevens T. Mason was the first state governor. Detroit was the first capital. Then, in 1847, Lansing became the capital, as it is today.

THE YOUNG WOLVERINE STATE

When Michigan became a state, Americans were arguing over slavery. The South allowed slavery. In Michigan and the other northern states, slavery was outlawed. Many northerners wanted the South to end slavery, too.

Michigan people are often called Michiganians.

Michigan was a strong antislavery state. Some Michiganians turned their homes into stops on the Underground Railroad. This was a series of hiding places for slaves who were escaping to Canada. At one house in Schoolcraft, more than four hundred escaped slaves were hidden at various times.

The arguing over slavery and other issues led to war. War between the Union (the North) and the Confederacy (the South) began in 1861. It is called the Civil War (1861-1865).

About ninety thousand Michigan men fought for the Union. Michigan troops captured Jefferson Davis, president of the southern states. By the time

the Union won the war, about fourteen thousand Michigan troops had died.

Meanwhile, treasures were being discovered in Michigan. In 1840, geologist Douglass Houghton found rich copper deposits in the Upper Peninsula. Soon, Michigan was the scene of a "copper rush." In the late 1800s, Michigan led the nation in mining copper and iron.

Michigan was also the top lumber-producing state in the late 1800s. Lumberjacks came by the thousands to chop down Michigan trees. Muskegon, Manistee, Manistique, Escanaba, Menominee, and Saginaw became big lumbering

Michigan lumberjacks posed for this picture in the mid-1880s.

21

towns. Michigan provided some of the wood and metal that built Chicago and many other cities.

The lumberjacks and miners boosted Michigan's population. By 1890, the state had 2.1 million people. Only eight states had more people by then.

AUTOMOBILES AND AIRPLANES

Henry Ford (standing) built this "999" racing car in 1901 and hired Barney Oldfield (seated) to drive it in a 5-mile race. Oldfield won the race and set a world record.

Just before 1900, a machine was invented that changed the world. It was the automobile. Many people in the United States, France, and Germany had a hand in its creation. Among them were Henry Ford, Ransom Olds, and Charles King of Michigan.

Henry Ford lived in Detroit. He finished his first automobile on June 4, 1896. It was too big to fit through the door of the shed in which he had built it. Ford picked up an axe and smashed down the wall of the shed. Then he drove his first car down Detroit's Grand River Avenue. Also in 1896, Charles King produced his first car in Detroit, and Ransom Olds produced a car in Lansing.

Thousands of people wanted cars of their own. Detroit became the nation's leading car-making city. In 1899, Ransom Olds founded the Olds Motor Works in Detroit. The Oldsmobiles made there were the first cars produced in large numbers. Carmaker David Buick founded the Buick Company in Detroit in 1902. The next year, Henry Ford began the Ford Motor Company in Detroit. A few years later, John and Horace Dodge founded the Dodge Brothers car firm near Detroit.

Oldsmobiles, Buicks, Fords, and Dodges are still popular cars.

The early cars cost a great deal. Only rich people could buy them. In 1908, Henry Ford developed his Model T Ford. It sold for just a few hundred dollars. The Model T helped put millions of Americans on wheels.

People flocked to Michigan in the early 1900s. They went there to work in the car plants and other factories. Many came all the way from Europe.

Michigan did much to help the United States and its allies win World War I (1914-1918). The state provided more than 135,000 troops. Detroit made airplanes, airplane engines, trucks, and tanks for the armed forces.

A few years after World War I ended, the Great Depression (1929-1939) began. This was a period of hard times for the nation. Millions of Americans lost their jobs and their homes. Michigan suffered terribly. Americans couldn't afford new cars. Thousands of auto workers and other factory workers had lost their jobs. By 1933, more than half the state's factory workers were unemployed.

World War II (1939-1945) helped pull the country out of the depression. The United States entered the war in 1941. Michigan sent nearly seven hundred thousand men and women off to war. Michigan also made more war supplies than any other state. The Ford Motor Company built thousands of B-24 bomber airplanes. Jeeps, tanks, machine guns, and torpedoes were also made in Michigan. Detroit made so many war materials that it was called the "Arsenal of Democracy."

MODERN TIMES

Traveling between the two sections of Michigan had always been difficult. Water separates the two peninsulas. The closest the two regions come to each other is at the Straits of Mackinac. There, they are 5 miles apart. People going between the two

Michigan made one-eighth of the nation's war supplies during World War II.

peninsulas had to take a ferryboat or make a long ride over land.

For years, people spoke of linking the peninsulas by bridge. This was done in 1957. In that year, the Mackinac Bridge across the Straits of Mackinac opened. Thousands of cars each day now roll over "Big Mac."

In 1974, a Michigan man became the thirty-eighth president of the United States. It happened in a strange way. In 1973, Spiro Agnew resigned as vice-president. President Richard Nixon chose Congressman Gerald Ford of Michigan as the new vice-president. When Nixon resigned in 1974, Ford became president. He served until 1977.

Michigan has had some big problems in recent years. One problem concerns race relations. Detroit has a large black population. Many black Detroiters

Only a handful of states have more black people than Michigan.

are very poor. They feel that white people have been unfair to them in many ways. At times, some black Detroiters have taken out their anger violently. In 1967, there was a riot in a mainly black part of Detroit. The rioters burned buildings. They shot at police and fire fighters. Forty-three people died. This was one of the worst race riots in American history.

Unemployment is another Michigan problem. During much of the 1980s and 1990s, Michigan has had one of the nation's highest unemployment rates. By late 1990, more than seven of every one hundred Michigan workers were jobless. Only three states had a larger percentage of people who were out of work. A big reason for this is that the auto industry has slowed down in recent times.

Business has been poor in Michigan partly because of the state's high taxes. Recently, Michigan has been working to lower its taxes. Michiganians hope that will attract more business. More industry would mean jobs for thousands of Michiganians.

Education is another big issue in Michigan today. The state plans to increase funding for its schools in the 1990s. The added funds could reduce class sizes and improve the state's schools in many other ways.

Michiganians and Their Work

MICHIGANIANS AND THEIR WORK

As of 1990, 9.3 million people lived in Michigan. Only seven states had more people. Michigan's people come from many different backgrounds. About 1.3 million of them are black. Large numbers of Michiganians, or their ancestors, came from Canada. Many others are of German, Irish, Dutch, Polish, Italian, Russian, Finnish, and Swedish ancestry. Michigan is also home to about sixty thousand Native Americans. Some of them live on reservations.

Opposite: Girls picking strawberries

Michigan's people come from many different backgrounds.

These are lands that have been set aside for Native Americans. One reservation is the Saginaw-Chippewa Tribal Indian Reservation in the Lower Peninsula. Another is the Sault Sainte Marie Reservation in the Upper Peninsula.

Making products in factories is the main kind of work in Michigan. One-fourth of the state's workers make products. Motor vehicles are Michigan's number-one product. They include cars, trucks, and buses. Other major products include computers and other machinery, tools and other metal goods, furniture, paper, sports equipment, and medicine.

Michigan is also a big food packager. Kellogg, Post, and Ralston Purina make breakfast cereals in

Motor vehicles are Michigan's number-one product. This man is working on a General Motors assembly line.

Battle Creek. Gerber Foods has a huge baby-food factory in Fremont. Michigan also packages a lot of sugar.

Many Michiganians provide services for a living. For example, more than a million Michiganians work for the government. Only a handful of states have more government workers. Since Michigan is a vacationland, thousands of its people work in hotels and ski resorts. Many people work in banks in Detroit, which is a big financial center.

About fifty-four thousand Michigan families live on farms. Nearly all of the farms are in the Lower Peninsula. Michigan is the top state for growing cherries, dry beans, cucumbers for pickles, and blueberries. In addition, Michigan is a leader in growing apples, corn, grapes, soybeans, strawberries, sugar beets, and Christmas trees. Each winter, millions of Michigan Christmas trees are shipped around the country. Only six states produce more milk than Michigan. The state's farmers also raise hogs and turkeys.

Mining is not as important to Michigan as it once was. Yet, a great deal of iron and copper are still mined in the state. These metals come from the Upper Peninsula. Oil and salt are found in the Lower Peninsula.

Michigan is a leader in growing many kinds of fruit, especially apples (above) and cherries (below).

A Trip Through Michigan

A TRIP THROUGH MICHIGAN

Michigan is a great state to visit. Few states offer as much variety. The Wolverine State has big cities and lovely farms. It has more than 3,000 miles of Great Lakes beaches. The state also has vast woodlands and interesting wildlife.

Pages 32-33: The Grand Hotel, Mackinac Island

DETROIT

Detroit would be a good place to begin a trip through Michigan. The city is in the southeastern Lower Peninsula. It lies on the Detroit River just across from Windsor, Ontario, in Canada. Antoine de la Mothe Cadillac felt that he had picked a good spot when he founded Detroit in 1701. He was right. Detroit today has more than a million people. Only six cities in the United States have more people than Detroit. About half the people in all of Michigan live in the Detroit area.

Detroit's nearness to water helped it grow. The Detroit and St. Clair rivers link the city with the Great Lakes. Products can go by ship between Detroit and other cities along the Great Lakes.

The Detroit skyline

Chemicals, tools, and business machines are made in Detroit. But cars are the city's main product. Detroit is called the "Motor City" because it is America's top car-making center.

Several automakers offer tours that show how cars are produced. Detroit's tallest building is another highlight of the city. It is a seventy-three-story hotel. The hotel is part of a group of buildings called the Renaissance Center. Windsor, in Canada, can be seen from the hotel tower.

Before the Civil War, escaping slaves called Windsor the "Promised Land." Once there, they were free. Detroit's Museum of African History has

Left: Detroit's Renaissance Center opened in 1977. Right: Sparks shower from a body-welding section of a "Motor City" assembly plant.

This man at Detroit's historic Fort Wayne is dressed as a soldier of the Civil War era.

Scott Fountain (below) is in Detroit's Belle Isle Park.

displays on Michigan's role in the Underground Railroad.

Detroit has other fine museums. The Detroit Historical Museum has a display called "Streets of Old Detroit." The display shows what the city was like in the 1800s. The Detroit Institute of Arts has paintings by Rembrandt, Van Gogh, and other great artists. Fort Wayne, in Detroit, is 150 years old. It is one of the nation's best-kept old forts. A museum in the fort has displays on the city's military history.

Detroit has an unusual park on an island in the Detroit River. Called Belle Isle Park, it has an aquarium and a children's zoo. For music lovers, Detroit has a fine symphony orchestra and an opera. Detroit

is also a sports center. The Tigers are Detroit's major-league baseball team. The Lions are its pro football team. The Red Wings are its pro hockey team. The Pistons are the Motor City's famous pro basketball team.

THE SOUTHERN LOWER PENINSULA

Several cities near Detroit also make cars and car parts. They include Pontiac, Flint, and Dearborn. The Ford Motor Company's main factory is in Dearborn, which was where Henry Ford was born. His fifty-six-room home in Dearborn is open to visitors. It is called Fair Lane. Henry Ford also founded Greenfield Village in Dearborn. It has many historic buildings. For example, inventor Thomas Edison's laboratory was moved to Greenfield Village from New Jersey. The nearby Henry Ford Museum includes displays on inventions, bicycles, cars, and airplanes.

Four important cities lie west of Detroit. The first of these is Ann Arbor. Founded in the 1820s, Ann Arbor was named for either Ann Rumsey or Ann D'Arbeur. They were pioneers in the area. Ann Arbor is home to the University of Michigan. It is one of the nation's best universities.

Above: A millinery (hat) shop at historic Greenfield Village, in Dearborn
Below: The Student Union at the University of Michigan in Ann Arbor

The Democratic party is the country's other major political party.

Jackson is west of Ann Arbor. In 1854, some people who hated slavery met in Jackson. They helped organize a new political party. They called it the Republican party. Today, the Republican party is one of the nation's two main political parties. The Michigan Space Center is a highlight of Jackson. It has rockets, moon rocks, and other displays on space travel.

Battle Creek is west of Jackson. In the late 1800s, John and William Kellogg of Battle Creek grew interested in health foods. John Kellogg was a physician. The Kellogg brothers created new breakfast cereals. Charles Post was a patient of Dr. Kellogg's. He shared the Kellogg brothers' interest in health foods. Around the year 1900, Charles Post and William Kellogg formed cereal companies. The Kellogg and Post companies helped make Battle Creek the "Cereal Bowl of America." No other city on earth makes as much breakfast cereal as Battle Creek.

Kalamazoo is west of Battle Creek. The city's name comes from the Indian word *Kikalemazo*. It means something like "bubbling water," referring to the Kalamazoo River. Kalamazoo is home to Western Michigan University. The Kalamazoo Aviation History Museum has many old airplanes.

Grand Rapids is an hour's drive north of Kalamazoo. Fur trader Louis Campau founded Grand Rapids in 1826. Today, Grand Rapids is Michigan's second-largest city, behind only Detroit. Office furniture, shoes, and household-care items are made in the Grand Rapids area.

President Gerald Ford grew up in Grand Rapids. The city's Gerald R. Ford Museum has displays on his life. The museum has a full-size reproduction of Ford's White House office.

Lansing, the state capital, is east of Grand Rapids. In the 1840s, Michigan lawmakers decided

The State Capitol, in Lansing

to move the capital away from Detroit. They wanted a capital nearer the center of the state. The lawmakers argued over where it should be. Finally, someone said Lansing—perhaps as a joke. Lansing had one log house and a sawmill at the time. Yet, the lawmakers chose Lansing, which has been the capital since 1847.

The state capitol in Lansing is where Michigan lawmakers meet. It looks much like the United States Capitol in Washington, D.C. The Michigan Historical Museum is near the capitol. It has displays on Michigan history. The Michigan Women's Hall of Fame in Lansing honors famous women from the Wolverine State.

Lansing was where Ransom Olds built his first Oldsmobiles. Today, cars, auto parts, and scientific instruments are made in Lansing. Michigan State University is nearby in East Lansing.

The Michigan town of Holland is famous for its Tulip Festival.

The southern Lower Peninsula has many interesting small towns. Holland, a town near Lake Michigan, was founded in the 1840s by Dutch people. The town has a two-hundred-year-old windmill that was sent from The Netherlands. Each spring, Holland hosts its famous Tulip Festival. The townspeople dress in traditional Dutch clothing and dance in wooden shoes.

The southern Lower Peninsula has many farms. The strip of land along Lake Michigan is a big fruit-growing region. Huge harvests of cherries, apples, and other fruits come from this area. Michigan grows 150 million pounds of cherries a year. This comes to 10 billion cherries—40 for each person in the United States.

THE NORTHERN LOWER PENINSULA

Alpena, a town on Lake Huron, has an unusual offshore "museum." It is called the Thunder Bay Underwater Preserve. Divers come here to explore shipwrecks at the bottom of Lake Huron.

Interlochen, near Traverse City, is home to the Interlochen Center for the Arts. Young people at this famous year-round school study such subjects as music, dance, writing, acting, and painting.

Dutch people are from The Netherlands, a European nation that is also called Holland.

There is a town called Fruitport along Lake Michigan.

41

Left: People climbing Sleeping Bear Dune Right: A musket demonstration at Fort Mackinac

Sand dunes are hills of sand that have been piled up by the wind.

There are many vacation resorts along the Lower Peninsula's lake shores. Petoskey, Harbor Springs, and Boyne City are resort towns in the north. Skiers come to this area in the wintertime. Summer visitors come to swim and sail.

The Lake Michigan shore is known for its sand dunes. Sleeping Bear Dune is a sand hill that is nearly 500 feet tall. It looks like a bear taking a nap. From the top of the dune, North and South Manitou islands in Lake Michigan can be seen.

Many islands off the Michigan shore can be reached by ferryboat. One of them is Mackinac Island. It lies between the two peninsulas. Cars are not allowed on Mackinac Island. People on the island walk, bike, or travel by horse-drawn buggy. Fort Mackinac was built on Mackinac Island by the British in 1780. It is now a living-history museum.

THE UPPER PENINSULA

Cars use the Mackinac Bridge to travel between the Lower Peninsula and the Upper Peninsula. The Upper Peninsula can also be reached by boat or by driving through Wisconsin.

The Upper Peninsula is a world apart from Lower Michigan. To start with, it has far fewer people. Only about 315,000 people live in the Upper Peninsula. Detroit alone has more than three times that many people. The Upper Peninsula's biggest city, Marquette, has only 22,000 people. If it were near Detroit, Marquette would just be a small suburb.

The Upper Peninsula is very beautiful. It has sparkling streams. It has air so clear that on summer nights, the Milky Way seems close enough to touch. And it has vast woodlands where people camp and hike.

Porcupine Mountains Wilderness State Park attracts many hikers. The Porkies, as these mountains are called, are rugged and beautiful. Lake of

The Mackinac Bridge across the Straits of Mackinac links the Upper Peninsula and the Lower Peninsula.

the Clouds is in the Porkies. Its quiet waters reflect the sky like a huge mirror.

The Upper Peninsula has many skiing areas. Big Powderhorn Mountain and Indianhead Mountain are famous ski resorts. Copper Peak has the world's largest man-made ski slide. From the top of Copper Peak, visitors can see across Lake Superior to Canada.

Because of its mountains and streams, the Upper Peninsula has many waterfalls. Upper and Lower Tahquamenon Falls are famed for their beauty. Whitefish Falls and Agate Falls are among Upper Michigan's 150 other waterfalls.

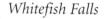

Whitefish Falls

The Upper Peninsula's woods and waters are home to a variety of wildlife. Deer can be seen darting through the woods. Black bears can be spotted in many places. Coyotes can sometimes be heard howling at night. Porcupines, bobcats, and beavers also live in the Upper Peninsula. Owls, bald eagles, and hawks are among the region's many birds.

The Hiawatha National Forest was the setting for Henry Wadsworth Longfellow's *Song of Hiawatha.* After this famous poem was published in 1855, the Upper Peninsula became known as the "Land of Hiawatha." The city of Ironwood has a huge statue of Longfellow's Hiawatha.

The Upper Peninsula is also called the "Treasure Chest" because of its iron and copper. Several old mines can be visited. Among them are

Bald eagles (left) and bobcats (right) can be seen in the Upper Peninsula.

Children learn to ski at Indianhead, one of the Upper Peninsula's many ski resorts.

the Iron Mountain Iron Mine at Vulcan and the Arcadian Copper Mine near Hancock.

Mining is less important to Michigan than it once was. But tourism has grown in importance. Many people in the Upper Peninsula work at ski resorts and motels.

Some of the Upper Peninsula's loveliest areas can be reached by boat. Pictured Rocks National Lakeshore is on the Lake Superior shore near Munising. The Pictured Rocks are beautiful when seen from the water. These colorful cliffs were carved by glaciers and waves over millions of years.

Boats and seaplanes take people to Lake Superior's Isle Royale. Moose and wolves live on this island. In 1912, Lake Superior froze over. It is thought that wolves and moose reached the island by crossing on the ice from Canada.

Sault Sainte Marie is a good place to finish a Michigan trip. The city is on the Saint Marys River. Its twin city, Ontario's Sault Sainte Marie, is across the river in Canada. Many people call the city "the Soo."

Begun in 1668, the Soo is the state's oldest town. The Bishop Baraga House Museum was the home of Bishop Frederic Baraga (1797-1868). He was a pioneer priest in the area. Baraga was called

the "Snowshoe Priest" because of how he traveled in the wintertime.

The famous Soo Canals and Locks are at Sault Sainte Marie. The first canal was completed in 1855. The canals solved an old problem. The Saint Marys River links Lake Superior with nearby Lake Huron. But Lake Superior's waters are 20 feet higher than those of Lake Huron. Traveling on the St. Marys River between the two lakes was a little like going over a waterfall. The canals and locks raise and lower ships so they can pass between Lakes Superior and Huron. Each year, thousands of ships pass through these canals.

Two of the sights at Pictured Rocks National Lakeshore are the rock called Miner's Castle (left) and the miniature waterfall at Miner's Beach (right).

A Gallery of Famous Wolverines

A GALLERY OF FAMOUS WOLVERINES

Michigan has been home to many famous people. They range from fur traders to basketball stars. **Antoine de la Mothe Cadillac (1658?-1730)** was born in France. He came to Canada when he was about twenty-five. Cadillac is best known for founding Detroit. His writings tell us what Michigan and its Indians were like around the year 1700.

Lewis Cass (1782-1866) was born in New Hampshire. After serving as a soldier, he became governor of the Michigan Territory. Cass served as Michigan's governor for eighteen years. During that time, he built roads, explored Michigan, and obtained land from the Indians. After Michigan became a state, Cass became a U.S. senator.

Stevens T. Mason (1811-1843) was born in Virginia. He came to Michigan in 1830. His father served briefly as the territory's governor. Mason helped his father with his work. Stevens T. Mason became the Michigan Territory's acting governor in 1831. Since he was only nineteen years old, he was called the "Boy Governor." Later, Mason was elected Michigan's first state governor.

Lewis Cass

Opposite: Charles Lindbergh with the Spirit of St. Louis

Whooping cough is sometimes called pertussis. The "p" in DTP stands for pertussis.

Ralph Bunche (above) helped found the United Nations. It is an organization that works for world peace.

Pearl Kendrick (1890-1980) was born in Illinois. **Grace Eldering** (1900-1988) was born in Montana. Both women became doctors. They went to work for the Michigan Department of Health. Drs. Kendrick and Eldering began searching for a way to prevent whooping cough. This disease claimed thousands of young lives during the 1930s. In 1939, the two doctors developed a vaccine to prevent whooping cough. They then developed the DTP vaccine. One single DTP shot protects against diphtheria, whooping cough, and tetanus. The work of Drs. Kendrick and Eldering has saved countless young lives around the world.

Ralph J. Bunche (1904-1971) was born in Detroit. He became a famous statesman. Bunche helped found the United Nations (UN). While working for the UN, Bunche helped make a peace agreement between the Arabs and the Jews in the Middle East. In 1950, Bunche became the first black American to win the Nobel Peace Prize.

Gerald Ford was born in Omaha, Nebraska, in 1913. He moved with his mother to Grand Rapids, Michigan, when he was two. Ford went to the University of Michigan. He was a football star at the university. Later, he entered politics. Ford was a member of the U. S. House of Representatives from

1948 to 1973. He was appointed vice-president of the United States in 1973 and became president in 1974.

Charles Lindbergh (1902-1974) was born in Detroit. When he was in his early twenties, Lindbergh began flying airplanes. He became a great flyer. In 1927, he became the first pilot to make a nonstop, solo flight across the Atlantic Ocean.

Coleman Young was born in Alabama in 1918. He moved to Detroit when he was five years old. Young was elected mayor of Detroit in 1973. He became the city's first black mayor. By 1991, Young had been mayor of the Motor City for nearly twenty years.

The Wolverine State has produced some great authors. **Marguerite de Angeli** (1889-1987) was born in Lapeer. De Angeli became a famous author and illustrator of children's books. She won the 1950 Newbery Medal for *The Door in the Wall.* Her other works include *Elin's Amerika, Bright April,* and *Black Fox of Lorne.* Marguerite de Angeli lived to the age of ninety-eight.

The famous author **Edna Ferber** (1887-1968) was born in Kalamazoo. Several of her novels, including *Show Boat, Come and Get It,* and *Giant,*

Gerald R. Ford on a tennis court with his daughter, Susan

Edna Ferber

were made into fine films. **Bruce Catton** (1899-1978) was born in Petosky. He wrote books about the Civil War. His *Stillness at Appomattox* won the 1954 National Book Award.

Many great athletes have lived in Michigan. Boxer **Joe Louis** (1914-1981) was born in Alabama but grew up in Detroit. Known as the "Brown Bomber," Louis held the heavyweight title for twelve years—longer than any other man. Welterweight and middleweight boxing champ **"Sugar Ray" Robinson** (1920-1989) was born in Detroit. Basketball great **Earvin "Magic" Johnson** was born in East Lansing in 1959. He was pro basketball's most valuable player in 1987, 1989, and 1990.

Joe Louis

Earvin "Magic" Johnson

Michigan has also produced many famous entertainers. Singer and actress **Diana Ross** was born in Detroit in 1944. She led the singing group called the Supremes. She also starred in the film *Lady Sings the Blues.* Actor **Tom Selleck** was born in Detroit in 1945. He starred in the television series called "Magnum P.I." Singer and composer **Stevie Wonder** was born in Saginaw in 1950. Wonder, who is blind, recorded his first hit at the age of twelve. "You Are the Sunshine of My Life" is just one of the beautiful songs he has written and sung. **Madonna Louise Ciccone** was born in Bay City in 1959. Known simply as Madonna, she is a popular singer and actress.

Tom Selleck

Diana Ross

Home to Antoine de la Mothe Cadillac, Gerald Ford, Marguerite de Angeli, Ralph Bunche, and the "Boy Governor" . . .

The place where the Republican party was named, and where Henry Ford and Ransom Olds helped develop the automobile . . .

A land of beautiful lakes, mountains, waterfalls, islands, and forests . . .

A leader in producing cars, breakfast cereals, cherries, and apples . . .

This is the Wolverine State—Michigan!

Did You Know?

The world's first mile of concrete highway was laid in Detroit in 1908.

A Traverse City bakery made the largest cherry pie on record in 1987. It weighed 28,355 pounds (as much as three grown elephants) and was 17.5 feet in diameter. The pie was made for the National Cherry Festival that is held each year in Traverse City.

The famous Motown record company was founded in Detroit in 1959.

When Stevens T. Mason first became governor of the Territory of Michigan, the voting age was twenty-one. Mason was only nineteen. This meant that the governor was too young to vote.

There is a town near Saginaw with the strange name Zilwaukee. Its founders hoped that people would confuse the name with Milwaukee (in Wisconsin) and move to Zilwaukee by accident. The plan didn't work very well, for Zilwaukee has only about two thousand people.

After Michigan became a state in 1837, the United States adopted a new flag. It had twenty-six stars (one for each state) arranged in the shape of a big star.

President Gerald Ford was named Most Valuable Player on the University of Michigan's 1934 football team.

The carpet sweeper was invented in Grand Rapids in 1876 by M. R. Bissell.

Lansing's name was nearly changed to Michigan when it became the state capital. Had the change occurred, the capital would be Michigan, Michigan.

There is a town called Paradise in the Upper Peninsula.

There is a town called Hell in the Lower Peninsula. It is between Lansing and Ann Arbor.

Three Miss Americas have come from Michigan: Detroit's Patricia Donnelly (1939), Montague's Nancy Fleming (1961), and Birmingham's Pamela Anne Eldred (1970).

More than 15 million Model T Fords were sold between 1908 and 1927.

In 1905, the speed limit in Michigan for cars was twenty-five miles per hour on highways and eight miles per hour in towns.

The University of Michigan was the 1989 college basketball champion. Michigan State won the title in 1979.

MICHIGAN INFORMATION

Area: 58,527 square miles (twenty-third among the states in size)

Greatest Distance North to South:
215 miles (Upper Peninsula)
285 miles (Lower Peninsula)

Greatest Distance East to West:
335 miles (Upper Peninsula)
200 miles (Lower Peninsula)

Borders (Upper Peninsula): Canada and Lake Superior to the north; Canada and Lake Huron to the east; Wisconsin and Lakes Huron and Michigan to the south; Wisconsin and Lake Superior to the west

Borders (Lower Peninsula): Lakes Huron and Michigan to the north; Canada and Lakes Huron and Erie to the east; Ohio and Indiana to the south; Lake Michigan to the west

Highest Point: Mount Arvon, 1,979 feet above sea level

Lowest Point: 572 feet above sea level, along Lake Erie

Hottest Recorded Temperature: 112° F. (at Mio, on July 13, 1936)

Coldest Recorded Temperature: -51° F. (at Vanderbilt, on February 9, 1934)

Statehood: The twenty-sixth state, on January 26, 1837

Origin of Name: From *Michigama*, a Chippewa word meaning "great lake"

Capital: Lansing (since 1847)

Counties: 83

United States Representatives: 16 (as of 1992)

State Senators: 38

State Representatives: 110

State Song: "Michigan, My Michigan"

State Motto: *Si quaeris peninsulam amoenam, circumspice* (Latin, meaning "If you seek a pleasant peninsula, look about you")

Robin

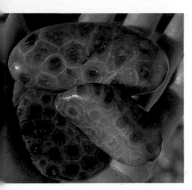

Petoskey stones

56

Nicknames: "Wolverine State," "Great Lakes State," "Water Wonderland"

State Seal: Adopted in 1835   **State Tree:** White pine

State Flag: Adopted in 1911   **State Fish:** Brook trout

State Flower: Apple blossom   **State Stone:** Petoskey

State Bird: Robin   **State Gem:** Isle Royale greenstone

Some Rivers: Grand, Kalamazoo, Saginaw, St. Clair, Manistee, Muskegon, Au Sable, Ontonagon, Escanaba, Manistique, Tahquamenon, St. Marys

Some Islands: Isle Royale, Mackinac, Drummond, Beaver, North Manitou, South Manitou

Some Waterfalls: Upper Tahquamenon Falls, Lower Tahquamenon Falls, Whitefish Falls, Agate Falls

Wildlife: Deer, black bears, badgers, bobcats, beavers, minks, porcupines, wolves, foxes, skunks, opossums, otters, raccoons, coyotes, ducks, geese, owls, bald eagles, hawks, many other birds

Fishing Products: Trout, herring, whitefish, perch, catfish

Farm Products: Cherries, apples, corn, blueberries, grapes, soybeans, strawberries, sugar beets, tomatoes, carrots, plums, peaches, wheat, Christmas trees, milk, hogs, turkeys, beef cattle

Mining: Iron, copper, salt, oil, natural gas, limestone, sand and gravel

Manufacturing Products: Cars, trucks, other motor vehicles, computers and other machinery, tools and other metal goods, furniture, paper, sports equipment, medicines, cement, breakfast cereals and many other foods

Population: 9, 295, 297, eighth among the states (1990 U.S. Census Bureau figures)

Major Cities (1990 Census):

Detroit	1,027,974	Sterling Heights	117,810
Grand Rapids	189,126	Ann Arbor	109,592
Warren	144,864	Livonia	100,850
Flint	140,761	Dearborn	89,286
Lansing	127,321		

White pine

Apple blossom

MICHIGAN HISTORY

About 10,000 B.C.—Prehistoric Indians live in Michigan

1620—Frenchman Étienne Brulé reaches Michigan around this time

1634—French explorer Jean Nicolet reaches Michigan

1660—Father René Ménard builds a mission at Keweenaw Bay

1668—Father Jacques Marquette founds Michigan's first non-Indian settlement at Sault Sainte Marie

1701—Antoine de la Mothe Cadillac founds Detroit

1750—Only about one thousand French settlers and soldiers live in Michigan by this time

1760—Rogers' Rangers seize Detroit for England during the French and Indian War

1763—The French and Indian War ends with the English in control of Michigan; the Indians fight Pontiac's War

1783—The United States wins the Revolutionary War; Michigan is part of the new nation

1787—Michigan becomes part of the Northwest Territory

1796—The English finally give up all their forts in Michigan

1805—The Territory of Michigan is created by the U.S. government

1825—The Erie Canal opens across New York State, making it easier to reach Michigan from the east

1837—Michigan becomes the twenty-sixth state on January 26; Detroit is the first state capital

1840—Dr. Douglass Houghton finds that the Upper Peninsula is rich in copper

1841—The University of Michigan opens at Ann Arbor

1844—Iron is discovered in the Upper Peninsula

1847—Lansing becomes Michigan's permanent capital

1854—The Republican party is named at a meeting in Jackson

Fayette State Park, a historic iron-ore smelting village, was founded in 1866. It was abandoned in 1890, and is now a ghost town.

1861-1865—Nearly 100,000 Michiganians fight for the North during the Civil War

1870—Michigan becomes the top lumber state; it holds the title for more than twenty years

1871—Forest fires sweep across Michigan

1896—Henry Ford of Detroit and Ransom Olds of Lansing finish building their first gasoline-powered cars

1899—Ransom Olds founds the Olds Motor Works in Detroit

1900—The population of the Wolverine State is 2.4 million

1908—Henry Ford starts making his Model T Ford

1917-1918—More than 135,000 Michiganians help the United States and its allies win World War I

1935—Auto workers organize the United Automobile Workers (UAW) union in Detroit

1937—The Wolverine State celebrates its 100th birthday

1941-1945—Nearly 700,000 Michigan men and women help the United States and its allies win World War II

1957—The Mackinac Bridge ("Big Mac") opens, linking Michigan's two peninsulas

1964—Michigan's current state constitution takes effect

1967—Forty three people die in a Detroit race riot

1973—Coleman Young is elected Detroit's first black mayor

1974—Gerald Ford of Michigan becomes the thirty-eighth president of the United States

1990—The population of the Wolverine State reaches 9.3 million

These members of the Michigan 4th Infantry served in the Civil War.

	1	2	3	4	5	6	7

A

Isle Royale

B

Hancock
Houghton
Keweenaw Bay
LAKE SUPERIOR

CANADA

Lake of the Clouds

Porcupine Mountains
Wilderness State Park
Mount Arvon (1,979 ft.)

Upper Falls

Ironwood

Agate Falls

Marquette

Munising

Sault Sainte Marie

C

ONTONAGON RIVER

UPPER PENINSULA

ESCANABA RIVER

Hiawatha
National
Forest

MANISTIQUE RIVER

TAHQUAMENON

Lower Falls

Hiawatha
National
Forest

Drummond Island

WISCONSIN

Vulcan

Escanaba

St. Ignace

Mackinac Island

Straits of Mackinac

D

Menominee

North Manitou Island

Beaver Island

Harbor Springs

Petoskey

Boyne City

Vanderbilt

Alpena

South Manitou Island

E

Traverse City

MANISTEE RIVER

AU SABLE RIVER

Mio

LAKE HURON

Manistee

F

LAKE MICHIGAN

MUSKEGON RIVER

LOWER PENINSULA

SAGINAW RIVER

Bay City
Zilwaukee
Saginaw

Montague

Muskegon

G

Fruitport

GRAND RIVER

Grand
Rapids

Holland

Flint

Lapeer

★ Lansing

Pontiac

Sterling
Heights

Birmingham

Warren

Livonia

Detroit

KALAMAZOO RIVER

Battle Creek

Dearborn

DETROIT
RIVER

H

Kalamazoo

Ann Arbor

Jackson

Schoolcraft

LAKE ERIE

INDIANA

OHIO

MAP KEY

Agate Falls	C2	Mount Arvon	C3
Alpena	D6,7	Munising	C4
Ann Arbor	H6	Muskegon	G4
Au Sable River	E6	Muskegon River	F4,5
Battle Creek	H5	North Manitou Island	D4
Bay City	F6	Ontonagon River	C2
Beaver Island	D5	Petoskey	D5
Birmingham	D7	Pontiac	G7
Boyne City	D5	Porcupine Mountains	
Dearborn	H7	Wilderness State	
Detroit	G,H7	Park	C1
Detroit River	H7	Saginaw	F6
Drummond Island	C6	Saginaw River	F,G6
Escanaba	D3,4	Sault Sainte Marie	C6
Escanaba River	C3	Schoolcraft	H5
Flint	G6	South Manitou Island	E4
Fruitport	G4	St. Ignace	D5
Grand Rapids	G5	St. Clair River	G7
Grand River	G5	Sterling Heights	G7
Hancock	B2	Straits of Mackinac	D5
Harbor Springs	D5	Tahquamenon River	C5
Hiawatha National		Traverse City	E5
Forest	C4, C5	Upper Tahquamenon	
Holland	G4	Falls	C5
Houghton	B2	Vanderbilt	D6
Ironwood	C1	Vulcan	D3
Isle Royale	A2	Warren	G7
Jackson	H6	Zilwaukee	F6
Kalamazoo	H5		
Kalamazoo River	G4,5		
Keweenaw Bay	B3		
Lake of the Clouds	B2		
Lake Erie	H7		
Lake Michigan			
	D,E,F,G,H3,4		
Lake Huron	D6,7;F,F7		
Lake Superior			
	B1,2,3,4,5,6		
Lansing	G6		
Lapeer	G7		
Livonia	G7		
Lower Tahquamenon			
Falls	C5		
Mackinac Island	D6		
Manistee	E4		
Manistee River	E5		
Manistique	C,D4		
Manistique River	C4,5		
Marquette	C3		
Menominee	D3		
Mio	E6		
Montague	F4		

GLOSSARY

allies: Nations that help one another

ancestor: A person from whom one is descended, such as a grandfather or a great-grandmother

ancient: Relating to those living at a time early in history

arsenal: A place where weapons are made or stored

billion: A thousand million (1,000,000,000)

capital: The city that is the seat of government

capitol: The building in which the government meets

century: A period of one hundred years

climate: The typical weather of a region

colony: A settlement outside a parent country and ruled by the parent country

explorers: People who visit and study unknown lands

geologists: People who study the history of the earth by studying the earth's rocks

manufacturing: The making of products

61

million: A thousand thousand (1,000,000)

mission: A place where religious work is carried on; a church

permanent: Lasting

population: The number of people in a place

prehistoric: Before written history

resign: To quit

snowshoes: Frames of wood that are strung with leather thongs; they are worn on the feet to help people walk on snow without sinking

solo: By oneself; alone

strait: A narrow body of water that connects two larger bodies of water

vaccine: A material that prevents disease; it is usually given as a shot (a vaccination)

PICTURE ACKNOWLEDGMENTS

Front cover, © Stephen Graham/**Dembinsky Photo Associates**; 1, © **SuperStock**; 2, **Tom Dunnington**; 3, © MacDonald Photography/**Photri**; 5, **Tom Dunnington**; 6-7, © Ron Goulet/**Dembinsky Photo Associates**; 8, © John Gerlach/**Dembinsky Photo Associates**; 9 (left), **courtesy Hammond, Incorporated, Maplewood, New Jersey**; 9 (right), © Tom Dietrich/**Tony Stone Worldwide/Chicago Ltd.**; 10 (left), © Ron Goulet/**Dembinsky Photo Associates**; 10 (right), © Ian J. Adams/**Dembinsky Photo Associates**; 11, © Ron Goulet/**Dembinsky Photo Associates**; 12, **AP/Wide World Photos**; 14, **State Historical Society of Wisconsin**; 15 (top), © **James P. Rowan**; 15 (bottom), © Gary Bublitz/**Dembinsky Photo Associates**; 17, **Historical Pictures Service, Chicago**; 19, **From the Collections of the Michigan State Archives, Department of State**; 21, **From the Collections of the Michigan State Archives, Department of State**; 22, **From the Collections of the Henry Ford Museum & Greenfield Village**; 24, **AP/Wide World Photos**; 25, **AP/Wide World Photos**; 26, © J. S. Sroka/**Dembinsky Photo Associates**; 28, © W. Metzen/**H. Armstrong Roberts**; 29 (left), © Larry Schaefer/**Root Resources**; 29 (right), © **Cameramann International, Ltd.**; 30, © **Cameramann International, Ltd.**; 31 (top), © Ron Goulet/**Dembinsky Photo Associates**; 31 (bottom), © B. Dimmick/**H. Armstrong Roberts**; 32-33, © **SuperStock**; 34, © W. Cody/**H. Armstrong Roberts**; 35 (left), © Michael E. Lubiarz/**Dembinsky Photo Associates**; 35 (right), © Andrew Sacks/**Tony Stone Worldwide/Chicago Ltd.**; 36 (top), © **James P. Rowan**; 36 (bottom), © D. E. Cox/**Tony Stone Worldwide/Chicago Ltd.**; 37 (top), © **James P. Rowan**; 37 (bottom), © Larime Photographic/**DembinskyPhoto Associates**; 39, © **SuperStock**; 40 (both pictures), © Stuart M. Williams/**Dembinsky Photo Associates**; 41, © Andy Sacks/**Tony Stone Worldwide/Chicago Ltd.**; 42 (left), © Joe Sroka/**Dembinsky Photo Associates**; 42 (right), © **Cameramann International, Ltd.**; 43, © **Cameramann International, Ltd.**; 44, © Ian J. Adams/**Dembinsky Photo Associates**; 45 (left), © Thomas Kitchin/**Tom Stack & Associates**; 45 (right), © Robert Winslow/**Tom Stack & Associates**; 46, © **Joan Dunlop**; 47 (left), © Ron Goulet/**Dembinsky Photo Associates**; 47 (right), © Ian J. Adams/**Dembinsky Photo Associates**; 48, **AP/Wide World Photos**; 49, **Historical Pictures Service, Chicago**; 50, **AP/Wide World Photos**; 51 (top), **Wide World Photos, Inc.**; 51 (bottom), **AP/Wide World Photos**; 52 (both pictures), **AP/Wide World Photos**; 53 (both pictures), **AP/Wide World Photos**; 54 (top), **Wide World Photos, Inc.**; 53 (bottom), **Michigan Cherry Committee**; 55 (left), **College Football Hall of Fame**; 55 (right), **AP/Wide World Photos**; 56 (top), **Courtesy Flag Research Center, Winchester, Massachusetts, 01890**; 56 (middle), © Rob Planck/**Dembinsky Photo Associates**; 56 (bottom), © Mary A. Root/**Root Resources**; 57 (top), © **Jerry Hennen**; 57 (bottom), © **Virginia R. Grimes**; 58, © **SuperStock**; 59, **From the Collections of the Michigan State Archives, Department of State**; 60, **Tom Dunnington**; back cover, © John Gerlach/**Dembinsky Photo Associates**

Index

Page numbers in boldface type indicate illustrations.

ABOUT THE AUTHOR

Dennis Brindell Fradin is the author of more than one hundred published children's books. His works for Childrens Press include the Young People's Stories of Our States series, the Disaster! series, and the Thirteen Colonies series. His other books are *Remarkable Children* (Little, Brown) and *How I Saved the World* (Dillon). Dennis is married to Judith Bloom Fradin, a high-school English teacher. They have two sons, Tony and Mike, and a daughter, Diana. Dennis graduated from Northwestern University in 1967 with a B.A. in creative writing, and has lived in Evanston, Illinois, since that year.